Mourant Brock

The cross, Heathen and Christian

A Fragmentary Notice of its Early Pagan Existence and Subsequent

Christian Adoption

Mourant Brock

The cross, Heathen and Christian
A Fragmentary Notice of its Early Pagan Existence and Subsequent Christian Adoption

ISBN/EAN: 9783337252472

Printed in Europe, USA, Canada, Australia, Japan

Cover: Foto ©Lupo / pixelio.de

More available books at **www.hansebooks.com**

THE CROSS:

HEATHEN AND CHRISTIAN.

A FRAGMENTARY NOTICE OF ITS EARLY PAGAN
EXISTENCE, AND SUBSEQUENT CHRISTIAN
ADOPTION.

WITH ILLUSTRATIONS.

BY

MOURANT BROCK, M.A.

SEELEY, JACKSON, AND HALLIDAY, 54, FLEET STREET,
LONDON. MDCCCLXXIX.

Price 1s. 6d.

TO CROSS WEARERS,

BEARERS,

AND TO THOSE WHO TAKE UP THE CROSS,

THIS FRAGMENT ON THE CROSS IS BY

AN OLD CROSS BEARER

(NOT WEARER),

Respectfully Dedicated.

NOTICE.

THIS FRAGMENT, which in fragments has already appeared in a London journal, was undertaken by the writer at the solicitation of a friend, who repeatedly urged him to write on this and on a larger subject—"Rome Pagan, and Rome Papal."

Composed at different times and places, there may be found in the FRAGMENT some want of coherence.

Disinclined to the work, and to the trouble necessarily by such a subject entailed, with reluctance he has yielded to pressure put upon him.

The result, in part, is the subsequent sheets, which, if God give ability, will be followed by an illustrated work on the subject above referred to, years ago planned, and now far advanced, of which this little volume properly forms a part.

To *the Cross*, in its historic and antiquarian aspect, the writer's mind has only been more recently turned, and that first by an observation on its comparatively modern church introduction in Dean Burgon's "Letters from Rome."

If the result of the labour subsequently spent in the investigation of the subject equals in any degree, to the benefit of some, the sanguine expectation of the writer's late friend, he will indeed be thankful.

M. B.

P.S.—Absence from books, at this great distance from home, precludes the possibility of finally comparing proof-sheets with the volumes referred to.

MENTONE, 1879.

POSTSCRIPT TO PAGE 66.

Subsequently to seeing the rude cuts in BARONIUS' great work, reproduced at page 66, a visit to the Oratory of *Sa. Maria in Comodim* (an ancient Baptistry *in Ravenna*) enables me to explain what from the Cardinal I could not well understand, namely, what some of the Emperors are represented as carrying in their right hand.

This, then, is not the *mappa*, or cloth, they used to throw down at the public games, but is a roll, or *rolume*.

RAVENNA was for some time the seat of the later Roman Empire, and is now celebrated, among other things, for its early *Christian Mosaics* (wall pictures in coloured stone, or glass) representing to a certain extent the costumes and customs of that day. There, in the Church of S. Vitale, may now be seen the Emperor JUSTINIAN (A.D. 547) with his Empress THEODORA, surrounded, respectively, by priests and ladies, in full costume, and, no doubt, portraits.

These mosaics, executed originally by artists from Constantinople, are the oldest and finest in Europe.

The one in question, which illustrates BARONIUS, is in the vault, or ceiling, of the above-named Baptistry, of which at Ravenna there are several. This one is of the sixth century. In the centre of the ceiling is represented the baptism of Christ. Around are the Apostles, each bearing a crown, with the exception of St. Peter and St. Paul, the former having in his hand the keys, the latter *a volume*.

From this work of art, compared with the cuts in BARONIUS of early Christian Emperors, it would appear that it was the custom of those ages to represent great men and persons of education in this peculiar manner.

Thus the Imperial coins and the vault of this Baptistry illustrate each other.

Ravenna, Hotel Spada d'Oro,
  May 28, 1879.

THE CROSS:

PAGAN AND CHRISTIAN.

———∞⚬∞———

I.

THE subject of this fragment is *The Cross*—the Cross which, rightly or wrongly, we have been accustomed to look upon as an exclusively *Christian* emblem.

But, Is it so?

We are constrained to reply in the negative, and to say that Heathenism, not Christianity, is its original possessor.

The Christian shares it only in common with the Pagan.

"The Cross is found on *Greek* pottery, dating from B.C. 700 to B.C. 500; and is, of the same date, found among the *Latin* race. In *India* it is found before the Christian era as a symbol of Buddha." — (*Ceramic Art*, by Waring, fol. : Day, 1874.)

1

In *Thibet* also it is found, in *Scandinavia*, and in the *North*. "These crosses (of varied fashions) thus exhibit forms of older and widely-spread Pagan symbols of deity, of sanctity, eternal life, and blessing, which can be traced from the East, *all over European lands*, Keltic and Gothic.' — (*Ibid*. pp. 10 —12.

See also Professor Wilson on Hindu sects, in " Asiatic Researches."

"The Abbé Pluché says that the *Egyptians* marked their god Canopus with a Tau, **T**." The vestments of the priest of Horus are covered with Crosses of equal limbs, thus **+**. The Cross is also the recognised sign of orthodox Buddhism. (See Waring : plate 39.)

These same shaped Crosses I have also observed in the Vatican Etruscan Museum, at Rome. They are on the breast of some large Etruscan male figures in paint, very pronounced, from mural decorations in ancient Etruscan tombs.

Similar also to these are Crosses on two figures (also on the breast) to be seen in the British Museum, in the great Egyptian Hall on the ground-floor, on the right, passing to the staircase. The picture (small) is from a wall at Thebes, and represents *Asiatics* bearing tribute. The Cross is the same shape as the above, of equal limbs.

There is a figure of the youthful Bacchus, taken

from an ancient vase with which antiquarians are familiar, holding a cup and a leafless branch—a figure of much beauty. The head-dress is a band ornamented with Crosses of the same form as above. A portion of the band falls from the head, and with its *fringe* and *single Cross*, if lengthened, would form curiously enough, a complete priest's stole.

Dr. Smith figures it in his "Dictionary of Antiquities," under article "Cantharus."

In the British Museum upstairs (ancient pottery), under glass, at the left, entering, are various examples—*vases*, *paterœ*, etc., of pre-historic pottery, many of which have on them Crosses of various forms and devices.

The Crosses in gold, found by Dr. Schliemann in the tomb at Mycenœ, he describes as numerous. The Greeks, as well as the Etruscans, therefore, used the sacred sign.

Fancy the Greek Achilles, Ajax, Ulysses, going forth to war bedecked like some modern Dora, Lydia, or Mary, with crosses:

> "Now a gilt Cross on Dora's prayer-book shines,
> As toward the church her solemn step inclines,
> Now from her neck one dangles in the dance,
> As if thereby she heavenward claimed advance."

And conceive Hector, with his Asiatic *confrères*,

1—2

ornamented in a similar way, meeting the Greek heroes! Why not? The Cross was more used at that time by the inhabitants of Asia than by those of Europe, and was to them, as to us, a *holy symbol*.

Only, do not let the Christians be selfish, and in their use of it exclude the Heathen, as the Heathen had the Cross at any rate 1000 years before them.

Do you doubt?

Nay, then go, I pray you, with me to our great National Museum in London, and there I will introduce you to an illustrious friend, SAMSI-VUL, son of *Shalmaneser*, king of Assyria, priest and king. We shall find him, as large as life, in stone, on the ground-floor, in a small room not far from another small room occupied by another friend (if so I may presume to call him) still more illustrious, the presiding *Genius loci*, the learned Interpreter of all the mighty wonders of the place.

I need not say I mean Dr. Birch, whose titles are as numerous as those of SAMSI-VUL, his honour much greater.

Well, SAMSI-VUL, son of *Shalmaneser*, what has he to do with Crosses?

Very much, seeing he wears suspended round his neck the very biggest and grandest Cross I ever there saw.

The Cross of Crosses is the Cross of SAMSI-VUL!

"*Pectoral*" is the proper ecclesiastical word, is it not? Well, as our friend, like the Pope, is an ecclesiastic, as well as a king, *Pectoral* will be the proper term. This *priest-king*, then, heathen though he be, wears like the Pope a *Pectoral*, wherein, as in many other respects, as we may see, the Pope resembles the Pagan: only, as before observed, the Pagan *in the way of antiquity* has the advantage of the Pope.

The Pope in the use of the Cross copies the Pagan, not the Pagan the Pope.

The best way will be to give the reader a representation of said *Pectoral*.

This grand *Pectoral* is exactly half the size of the original. In all other respects it is an exact representation. The image (in stone) is about life-size, or a little larger; so it may be easily judged how great a portion of the breast the Cross covers. It is in relief, standing out to about the thickness of a crown-piece, and like the whole image, is in wonderful preservation, for it goes back to between 800 or 900 years B.C., which is before the time of Isaiah.

Here it is, from a tracing I lately took on the spot.

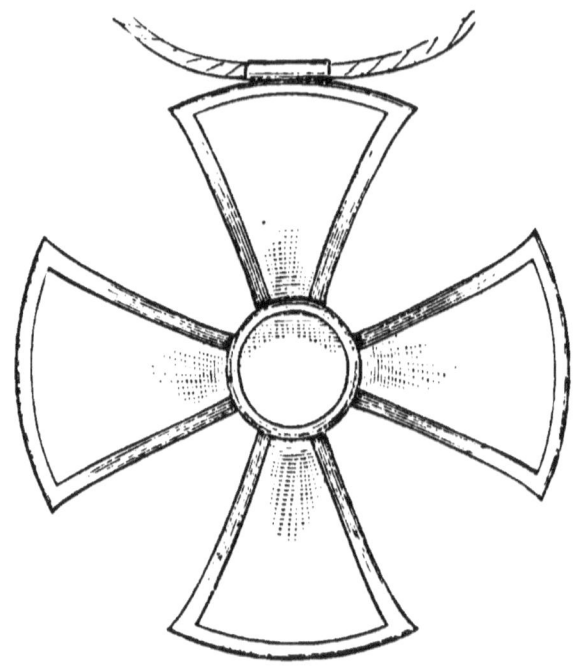

Cross worn by SAMSI-VUL IV., King of Assyria, B.C. 825.

Nor does this Cross stand alone as though it were an accidental ornament in Assyrian history, or rather in Assyrian *iconography*, or sacred signs. One finds it again, not to mention other examples, on the person of another Assyrian monarch, ASSUR-NAZIR-PAL, whose grand effigy in stone stands in the same suite of rooms.

The Crosses in both cases are alike.

Cross on the breast of Pio Nono's corpse as it "lay in state" at St. Peter's. The dotted lines are added to show its resemblance to the Cross of Samsi-Vul.

A fresh illustration of the early use of the Cross (also from Assyria) has recently been brought to light by M. Rassam's excavations, on the part of the British Museum, at Kalakh, an ancient capital of Assyria, on the east bank of the Tigris, twenty miles below Mosul.

This city was built by the Assyrian monarch, Assur-nazir-pal, who flourished from B.C. 885 to 860, as the arrow-headed inscriptions on the terracotta (burnt-clay) cylinders there found testify.

Happily for posterity, of this *most* enduring material were the libraries of kings and public records of Assyria usually formed.

"In the temple of the war-god, Adar, the *Mars* of the Assyrians, excavated in that city, M. Rassam found a number of very beautifully painted tiles, which had formed the bosses used to decorate the roof of this building, composed of fine clay; their surfaces had been enamelled, and on them were painted various geometrical patterns.

"The finest of these examples were in the shape of a Maltese cross."—(*Times*, Aug. 24, 1878.)

The tiles have pendants pierced for lamps, the ground a pale green, and in part richly gilt.

Thus, as many as over 860 years B.C., we have the Cross adorning the roof of a heathen temple on the banks of the Tigris.

But let me introduce the reader to another Cross, the one figured after that of SAMSI-VUL—the Cross of another Hierophant, of another Priest-king—the Cross of THE POPE OF ROME, Pio Nono.

There it is, as it was on his breast, as he " lay in state," in St. Peter's, as seen in the preceding page.

What a mockery to our lifeless humanity is that " lying in state !"

Well, poor old man ! there in St. Peter's, in January, 1878, he lay ; and comely in death he was with his nice benevolent face. I did not see him, but spoke with those who did. His photograph, which I got four months after in Rome, also now lies before me. So placid the face, and well formed! *Waxed,* however, it is. The Italians understand all this "get-up" and arrangement so well—filling up the wrinkles, setting the lips, etc. Then, mind also, one may *not come near.* Painted, too, it was most likely.

"Nonsense," do I hear you say? "Who ever heard of a corpse painted?"

Be not so hasty. I have seen a painted corpse.

I looked up in St. Peter's, where the old man lay, for I had ever a kindly feeling towards him, ever since, twenty-five years ago, sitting on his throne in the Sistine, surrounded by his masters, the cardinals, I saw him steal timid, furtive glances around. A deep impression did those furtive glances make on me of his helplessness and thrall.

Well, there he lay, high in air, some fourteen feet up, and over a vestry entrance, in a stuccoed tomb (till another is prepared), and where, I suppose, years ago, I saw his predecessor lie, before him.—They, you, and I, shall stand in the judgment.

People who were present in St. Peter's tell me that the poor old man's death was regarded by the people with entire indifference. While for King Victor Emmanuel, who lay dead at the same time, there was the expression of great sorrow, for Pio Nono none seemed to care.

It was so in Mendelssohn's time. He was at Rome at the period of the death of the then Pope, and in his published letters (well worth perusal), says that the Romans manifested the utmost indifference.

II.

But, the Cross?

He had many on him, like a priest of Isis—hands, feet, neck, breast, side, all were *crossed*. He was covered with this *charm*. The photo gives them.

But see how much his Cross resembles that of SAMSI-VUL. Widen the blades to the dotted lines, and it is the same thing. The Cross of the Pope is the Cross of the Pagan!

Yet, not far from a period of 3000 years has elapsed between the eras of these two Priest-kings. A wonderful continuity of *symbolism* is thus handed down from age to age, and that even to our own day !

Yes. But it admits of explanation. Both are Hierophants, observe, and administer much the same religious systems. Their succession also, from ancient times, is unbroken, even to the present day. Both are ministers of the *religion of Nature ;* both priests of the *Nature-goddess,* a worship which never fails. Their religion, then, being of the same type, there is no reason why their symbolism should differ.

Here may be suitably introduced the Crosses —forming another strange parallel, as the reader may judge—of two other personages, ladies this time : one from heathen mythology, the other from church iconography. ASTARTE, " Queen of Heaven," the Syrian or Phœnician Venus, is one, and ST. MARGARET—one hardly likes to name it—the fabled bride of Christ, is the other.

The latter, with her cross, is among representations of the saints often to be seen. This one is from Westminster Abbey. The former is not so frequent. Waring (plate 39) in his "Ceramic Art," has figured her, as in the woodcut below, enlarged from a coin. In the British Museum they have many of these *Astarte* coins, which were politely shown me, a cast of one of which I have now before me.

It will be seen how closely the Heathen and the Christian Cross resemble each other.

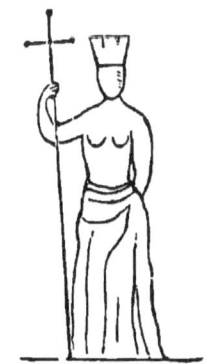

ASTARTE, the Syrian Venus.

ST. MARGARET.

Each of these ladies has also other attributes peculiar to herself, not here rendered.

Astarte, worshipped with rites obscene, or Ashtaroth, is that *Ishtar* whose descent and return from Hades is celebrated in Assyrian song, thus—

> " To the land of Hades
> Ishtar fixed her mind (to go)
> To the house of eternity,
> To the house men enter, but cannot depart from.
> To the road men go, but cannot return ;
> The abode of darkness and famine ;
> Light is not seen ; in darkness they dwell.
> Ghosts like birds flutter their wings,
> On the gate-posts dust lies undisturbed—
> When Ishtar arrived at the gate of Hades,
> To the keeper of the gate she spake :
> O keeper, open thy gate,
> Open thy gate, that I may enter."

So she enters. Of her jewels and clothing she is despoiled. The Queen of Hell gets in a tremendous passion, and is not very choice in her language. But the gods above cannot bear the absence of Ishtar. The earth droops and fades at her loss. The *Jove* of that mythology, *Hea*, therefore sends to fetch her by his messenger, *Phantom*. " Go, save her, Phantom," says he, "from the Queen of Hades." And this he does, by pleasing her with his mountebank tricks, such as " bringing fishes of the waters out of an empty vessel," etc.

So the Queen of Love is restored to gods above
and men below !

Thus far " The Legend of Ishtar," from the clay
tablet in the British Museum, marked K 162.

Under the name of *Hera*, Layard also (vol. ii.
p. 456), figures her from a rock-cut monument
holding a decorated Cross in the hand.

That the Cross is the received emblem of this
lewd Phœnician deity is further proved. Thus—

Roche, in his " Lexicon of Coins" (Lipsiæ, 1785),
under head *Astarte*, writes : " Illa succincta depin-
gitur aliquando caput *Osiridis* sustinens, aliquando
baculum *in crucem* efformatum."

And Eckhel (" Doctrina Nummorsum Veterum,"
iii. 371) has, "*Astarte* stans in templo tenens hastam
cum cruce."

Which may be thus rendered :

The former—She is represented girded, sometimes
bearing the head of Osiris, sometimes a rod shaped
as a Cross.

The latter—Astarte standing in a temple (so on
the coin represented), holding a lance with a Cross.

One is sorry to put " Maid Margaret, that was so
meek and mild " — *pearl* and *daisy*, for these her
name signifies—in such vile company. However,
we need not waste our sympathy, for no such person
(like St. Alban, also, as presumed) ever existed.

Even Pope Gelasius, Mrs. Jameson tells us, in 494, rejected her story as apocryphal.

So, adieu, Maid Margaret, "who upon the dragon stood."

As for "mooned Ashtaroth," perish her memory from the earth !

Let us now notice the universality of the use of the Cross.

All nations of antiquity, civilised or uncivilised, our own Druids included, delighted in the Cross. It seems to have been a sign connected with that *natural religion* which everywhere more or less underlies our humanity. Recently, the earth has given up a proof of its having been connected also with the sanguinary religion of ancient *Phœnicia*. An Aramæan seal of blue chalcedony was, December 5, 1876, lectured on at the rooms of the Society of Biblical Archæology, on which was a hieroglyphic figure with a crescent and a *Cross, crux ansata*, or *handled Cross*. On it was "an inscription in Phœnician characters of high antiquity," going back probably to the days, or beyond the days, of QUEEN DIDO, and connecting it with "a Chaldean lunar deity, Sin." (See Records of the Society.)

The *Phœnician*, as well as the *Assyrian* Astarte (Venus)—(see Layard)—are, we have seen, figured *holding a Cross*. In *India* it is also held in the hand by the gods of the country—Brama, Vishnu, etc. In Pagan *Mexico*, as well as in *China*, *Thibet*, and *Tartary*, the Cross is found. In Heathen China, as in Christian Europe, it is used *as a charm*. A consecrated wafer marked with a Cross was also used in the rites of Bacchus. The Cross in a circle is supposed to indicate sun worship.

The above particulars are from *Waring*.

Prescott thus informs us of the conversion of the Mexicans by the Spaniards from the worship of their *Rain-god*, whose emblem was a Cross:

"Their conversion went no further than the transfer of their homage from one Cross to another —from the Cross of their Rain-god to the same Cross as the emblem of Christ's salvation."—*History of Mexico*, 1,292.

Mr. Pascoe, now missionary in Mexico, thus confirms and enlarges on what Prescott tells us:

"The religion of the Mexicans was purely *Chaldean*. They professed to believe in a supreme God, but idol-worship was general. They had a regular *priesthood*, gorgeous *temples*, and *convents;* they had *processions* in which *Crosses*, and even red Crosses, were carried : and *incence, flowers,* and *fruit-offerings* were employed in their worship. They *confessed* to their priests, and generally confessed only once, receiving a written *absolution* which served for the

remainder of their lives as an effectual safeguard
against punishment, even for crimes committed *after
receiving* the said absolution. They worshipped,
and afterwards ate, a *wafer-god*, an idol made of flour
and honey, which they called 'the god of peni-
tence,' and they always ate *him fasting*. They also
venerated the black calf, or bull, and adored a
goddess-mother, with an *infant son in her arms*. They
sacrificed human victims to the God of Hell, of whom
they considered the Cross to be a symbol, and to
whom human victims were sacrificed, by laying them
on a great black stone and tearing out *their hearts.*"
(See Mr. Pascoe's speech at the Mildmay Confer-
ence, 1876.)

The Cross was also venerated by some of the
Mexican tribes, as the mark or symbol of their
great Messiah, whom they called Tamu.

In reference to the above-named "great black
stone" of human sacrifices, it is, I presume, the
same with those mentioned by Humboldt: "La
pierre dite des sacrifices, ornée d'un relief qui re-
présente le triomphe d'un roi Mexicain."

It is, he tells us, in area from eight to ten cubic
metres. (*Essai Politique*, etc., vol. ii. p. 120.) A metre
is a little over a yard. It is consequently vast.

"We saw," says Madame Calderon de la Barca
(Fanny Inglis — "Life in Mexico"), "the stone of
sacrifices now in the courtyard of the University

[of Mexico] with a hollow in the middle, in which the victim was laid."

Lately, at Lynmouth, in Devonshire (Sept., 1878), when paying a morning visit with the friend with whom I was staying, at Glenthorn, the beautiful and beautifully situated country seat of Mr. and Mrs. Halliday, I there saw a model, as I suppose, of this stone.

It was sent about twenty years ago to Mr. Halliday's predecessor, by the late Mr. F. Glennie, Consul at Mexico. It is in wax, excellently executed, circular, and on the drum of the circle, all round, is portrayed in low relief the "*triumph*," I presume, of which Humboldt speaks.

But this stone is remarkable for the number and form of the *Crosses* executed on it. Round the hollowed centre slaughter-cavity are circle after circle of, as it were, round shields in relief; then the external circle is formed of *Crosses* of this form, and many in number.

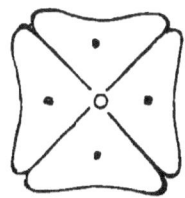

One of a circle of Crosses on the great stone altar at Mexico, for human sacrifices.

The ancient Mexicans are known to have largely

sacrificed human victims to their gods; and the Spaniards found in their day the horrid practice largely carried out.

Here then, in all probability, we have the savage and idolatrous rite of human sacrifices united to *their sacred emblem, the Cross.*

Prescott relates, that the victim being curved backward on the stone, the priest with a flint hatchet cut the breast of the victim open and tore out his heart, to be offered in sacrifice to the god of Hell or of War.

The lady to whom I have just alluded considers, and I think with great propriety, that the circle of Crosses formed by groups of four hearts (a Maltese Cross) represents hearts sacrificed to the gods; the dot on each specifies blood. In this case, each Cross forms four bleeding hearts.

" When Hernan Cortes and his handful of adventurers conquered Mexico in the sixteenth century, they found the introduction of their religion to be an easy matter. The simple method adopted in numerous cases by the priests in order to convert the Mexicans, was to remove by night the old Aztec idol from its niche, and place an image or painting of some Papal saint, or a *Crucifix*, in its stead. The next day the simple Indians would receive it as a divine miracle, and would at once render to the new god the worship they had so recently given to their old one.

"In this way was the change effected.

"Thus, the Papal sacrifice of the Mass replaced the old Aztec human sacrifices; and as the Mexicans were taught to believe that God's Son is literally slain thousands of times over in the course of a year, they readily accepted the substitution. Roman Catholic churches soon occupied the site of the old Aztec temples. Catholic priests and nuns replaced their Aztec predecessors. Processions still more pompous took the place of the old. Incense, flowers, and idols belonged to the new religion as to the old; even baptism and confession, and feasting on the wafer-god, were all continued, with but few, if any, improvements. The ancient *mother-goddess, whose statues yet remain*, gave way to the Papal Virgin-Mother with her child; *Crosses* became more numerous than ever; the same old familiar red Cross continued to be adored, with just one trifling change of title. What was once known as the mark of the god of Hell *now* became venerated as the sign of life, and the mark of the Papal Christian. The Indian Messiah Tamu was soon forgotten, and the Cross was now considered as a relic of the Apostle Thomas.

"Nor was 'the sacred heart,' or the black bull, discarded. The new religion gave him a place of honour in its festivals, and in many Papal churches in Mexico is he, to this day, worshipped as a black Messiah, with woolly hair and thick lips, and hanging on the Cross, his own especial symbol!"— *Pascoe.*

From the above we learn *certainly*—

1. That the *Cross* was of common use in the ancient Heathen rites of Pagan Mexico.

2. That the *Crosses* carved on the Mexican stone, sacrificial, altar represented, *possibly*, human hearts which were "*torn out*" of the murdered victims, and consecrated to their horrid gods.

In Catherwood's "Central America" are figured, I understand, many ancient Heathen Crosses. But I write this, far from books, *habitans in sicco.* Plenty of lemons, oranges, olives, and palms. But no books.

Much more remains to be said on the subject of the Crosses of Heathendom, a number of which, from different nations, will be seen in the next section.

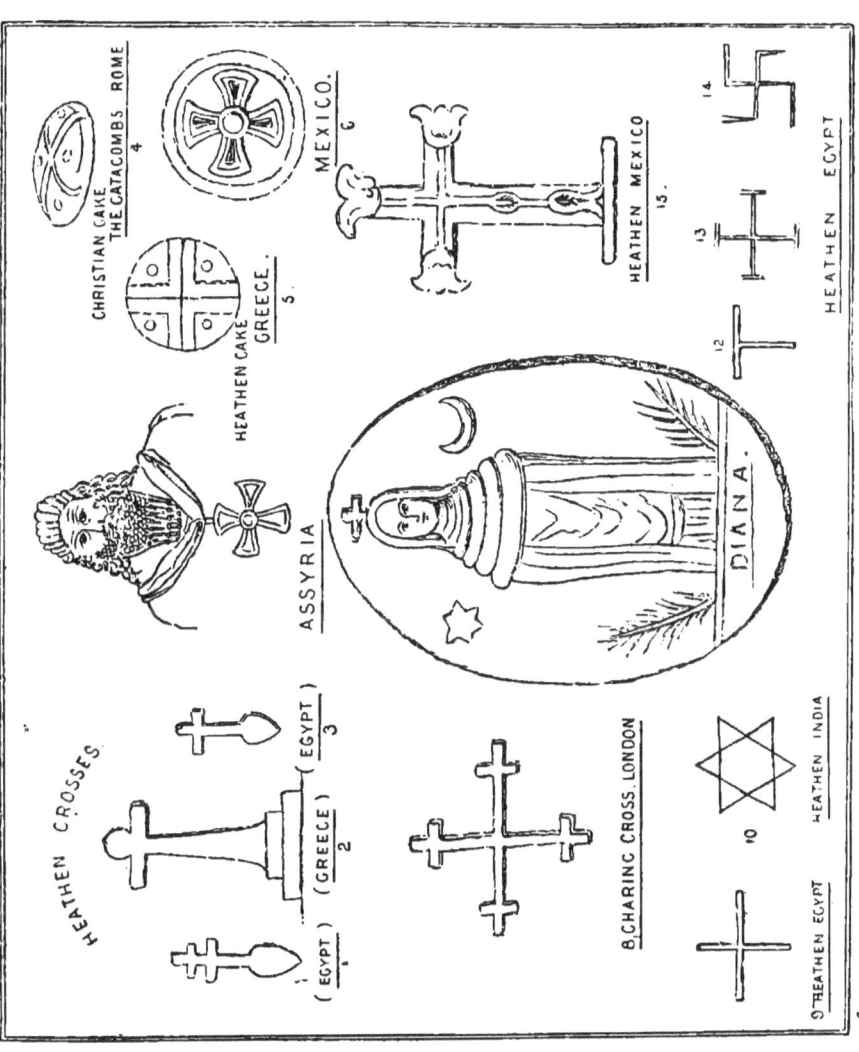

IV.

HERE are some of the Crosses alluded to. They
are mainly from heathen India, Assyria, Egypt,
Greece, and Mexico. Others might be added.
These, however, will suffice to show that the Cross
is not of Christian, but of Pagan origin.

Who would not suppose that the Cross was
Christian! The counterpart of those below, Heathen as they are, may be found in many of our
parish churches and churchyard crosses.

The following is an explanation of the cut :

On the breast of top centre figure is the Cross
pectoral of SAMSI-VUL, King of Assyria. It is, as
Dr. Birch informs me, the symbol of the god Annu.

Fig. 2 is a Greek cross from Thessaly, bearing
an inscription relating to funeral games.

Figs. 1 and 3 are Egyptian. They are, as may be
observed, a Cross fixed into a heart, or something
like a heart, and wonderfully similar to those vulgar,
red, blazing hearts one sees in Roman Catholic pictures with the Cross rising out of them—the *sacré
cœur*, connected with the fanatic M. Alacoque. Take
away the flames, and one might suppose the latter
had been taken from the former.

In Egyptian iconography (sacred writing) these *Cross* hearts are the *emblem of goodness.* In his "Ancient Egyptians" (vol. i. p. 7), Sir Gardner Wilkinson figures one of these emblems over the door of an ancient Egyptian house, which characterises it as "*the good house.*"

For all the world it is just like a modern "religious house" (*au bon Pasteur, e.g.*), so called.

Cross in bulb or heart, sign of " The Good House."—"Ancient Egypt."

Fig. 4. This is a Christian cake from the Roman Catacombs, and is, as may be observed, marked with a cross. It is like our " hot *cross buns,*" which indeed have a heathen origin, the word being derived from " *boun,*" a *sacred cake,* offered at the Arkite temples, every seventh day.

The Church cake, however, is also *a charm,* " will never grow mouldy, will ward off witches, sickness, and will protect the house from fire," etc.—(*Dictionary of Phrase and Fable.*)

Fig. **5,** which **4** resembles, is also a cake signed with the Cross, the same being consecrated to *Bacchus,* and used in his mysteries.

Cakes generally, whether signed or unsigned, were, and are, used in connection with the worship of the gods. Cecrops offered to *Jupiter* a sacred cake or *bun.* To *Hygea,* goddess of health, a similar offering was made, and the same to *Astarte* ("Mooned Asteroth, Heaven's queen and mother both") in Palestine, 600 years B.C. "The children gather wood, the fathers kindle the fire, and the women knead dough to *make cakes* to the queen of heaven" (Jer. vii. 18).

Nor, in connection with a religious rite, will it be forgotten that just prior to the Indian mutiny the cake was passed from hand to hand in India.

Two "cross buns," as used in the Bacchic orgies, were found at Herculaneum.

Fig. **6** is a stone Cross from heathen Mexico, figured by Lord Kingsborough in his great work on Mexico :

The large *medallion* is a curious figure. I took it at first for an archaic B. M. V., a rude representation of her! For there are two of her usual symbols—the sun and moon. Nor are the palm and the Cross unsuited to her iconography.

But, no. It is Diana! Who would have thought
it! So nearly does superstition make the Virgin-
Mother to resemble the ancient Virgin goddess.

The original is on a gem in the Naples Museum.

Fig. **8** is Charing Cross, as all will recognise, *i.e.*
the *chère Reine's* (dear Queen Eleanor's) Cross.
Chère Reine—Cha-ring.

Fig. **9** is an Egyptian Cross of very frequent
occurrence, and specially as belonging to the god
Horus, the vestments of whose priests were covered
with this sign.

Fig. **10**, not a cross, but a double triangle, is
from India, a sacred sign there.

We have largely adopted this Heathen emblem
in our sacred buildings, and elsewhere. It was
only the other day that in a village church I was
contemplating these two symbols (**9** and **10**) placed
near each other—*Heathen Egypt* and *Heathen India*
uniting their symbolism in an English parish
church! There was, besides, the *Indian nimbus*, or
glory—*three Heathen symbols* imported into a little
village church!

But that was not all, for I looked a little further,
and there were, as corbeilles on the pillars, *Heathen*
representations of winged Genii, *alias* Angels.

So here were *four* importations from Heathendom
in our little English church!

You will say, What matter? Who knows it?
May be so. But still, Heathenism it is, notwith-
standing, which thus invades our Christianity.

The *Crux ansata*, or Cross with a handle (*ansa*) is
not here figured.

In Egyptian symbolism it is the *emblem of life*,
and is commonly found in the hand of the king, as
also in India.

Fig. 12 is the well-known *tau*, or Greek T, with
which some will fabulate that the godly in Ezekiel's
vision (chap. ix.) were signed, and saved. Stevens
also gives it in his " Central America," and it is a
consecrated sign of the Egyptian Canopus god—as
also is Fig. 13.

Fig. 14 is the ancient, and universally spread, *Fyl-
fot*, called by French antiquarians *cramponnée*, or
cramped. The Scandinavians name it *the hammer
of Thor* (their god), or *Thor's hammer mark*.

To this form of the Cross we shall presently have
occasion again to refer.

Fig. 15, though like a decorated Latin Cross, is
also from *Heathen Mexico*, and figured by Stephens.

Most of the other Crosses may be found in
Waring's " Ceramic Art," before quoted.

The cut of B. M. V. following, adapted from the
Salisbury Chapter Seal given in the "Guide to
Salisbury," and of about the same size, is intended as

a pendant to DIANA at page 22, and should have come
on the following page. The agreement between the
symbolism of the two goddesses is remarkable.

To both are attributed the sun and moon. Both
have *the Sacred Cross*. The Christian divinity,
however, has one symbol over her compeer; she has
her *characteristic attribute* of the child, whom, as is
so frequently in Italian art represented, she suckles.

From Italy comes the ancient superstition, and,
as far as I know, from Italy comes also the ancient
art-symbolism. Hecate is *potent* in Earth, Hell,
and Heaven; but Mary almost, or quite, *omni-potent*.

From the Salisbury Chapter Seal.

V.

HAVING thus given some explanation of the several
Crosses marked in the preceding engraving, I add
some notice from Dr. Schliemann's "Troy" (Murray,
1875), of what he says of those Crosses, which in
his extensive explorations in the site of the old city
he has there discovered and subsequently figured.

These, for the most part found in very great
numbers, and of various forms, on objects in terra
cotta (*baked clay*), were dug up from a depth of from
two to fifty feet on the site of the ancient city, or
rather *cities*.

, Two forms are more common than others : the
croix cramponnée, which means *cramped* (see Fig.
14), called in Sanscrit (for the origin is Indian)
Suastika; and another Cross, called by the same
name, and of like shape. They were large "*fire
machines,*" the fire being produced by friction,
thus :

The cross-beams were placed on the ground hori-
zontally, and a piece of wood named *Pramantha*
dropped perpendicularly in a central hole, and
worked by a string, produced *the sacred fire*. This
fire was *a god* called *Agni*. His mother, *the Suastika,*
is the Indian *goddess,* *Maya*, Cybele, or Venus. They

are common, natural, and very ancient signs in India.
The footprints of *Buddha* (carved on the Amiaverti
Tope) are signed with them; and the prows of the
ships of King Rama, which over 1000 years B.C.
crossed the Ganges, were marked with this "holy
sign."

"From the very remotest times they were the
most sacred symbols of our Aryan forefathers."—
(*Edinb. Review*, Oct., 1870.)

Dr. Schliemann quotes as his authority for the
statements above made, as to the *Indian* parentage
of the Cross, the learned director of the French
school at Athens, Mons. Émile Burnouf, who is described by Mr. Smith, the editor of Dr. Schliemann's
work, as "possessing profound knowledge of Aryan
antiquities." From him the doctor quotes that the
Greeks derived the name and fable of *Prometheus*
from the above-named stake, *Pramantha*, the father
of the god, *fire*.

India, then, apparently, was the home of the Cross,
as it was of the *Nimbus* (see M. Didron, "Icono-
graphie Chrétienne"), whence both spread far and
wide.

It was a religious symbol of the very greatest
importance among the early progenitors of the
Aryan races. He tells us that in *Bactria* and in the
villages of the *Oxus* it has been dug up, also on
the right bank of the *Oder*. It is to be seen in

the British Museum on an ancient *Celtic* urn found
in Norfolk, and on many others.   It was a sign
of goodwill and luck.   The Trojans adopted it;
so also, in very early days, did the Greeks, as Dr.
Schliemann's recent excavations at the sepulchre at
Mycenæ prove.   The Greeks, who, like the Indians,
for a long time generated fire by friction, called the
transverse beams of the "Suastika," *stauros*, a Cross.
Then, ceasing to use them for fire purposes, the
word *stauros* (the New Testament term for the Cross
of our Lord) passed simply into the term " Cross."
(Schliemann's " Troy," pp. 101—105.)

VI.

Sufficient evidence, it is hoped, has now been ad-
duced to show that if Christians on their persons,
in their consecrated buildings, or elsewhere, choose
to use the Cross as a sacred emblem, they do so in
common with the Heathen of the past and of the
present.

In their simplicity the vast majority of Christians
suppose that the exclusive right to the Cross be-

longs to them, that it is exclusively a *Christian* emblem, that as a holy sign it derives its sanctity solely from *their* religion, and that it dates only from the *Christian era*.

The above facts put all these vain notions to flight.

If the Cross be adopted by the Christian, so was it long before by the Heathen. If it be holy to the one, so is it to the other. If it be a *charm* to chase evil from the home and person of the Christian, so it is used for the same purpose—and I may add, with the same success—to perform similar offices for the Gentile.

The Cross, of all religious emblems, is apparently the most ancient, as well as the most universal.

Evidently (why, we know not) the symbol of the Cross forms, with images, charms, fetish, pilgrimage, and other developments, one of those symbols which in every age, and through every land, manifest the existence of a religion universal, common to us all— the religion of the fleshly man. In other words, *the religion of nature*, which we call *Heathenism*.

As we recede from this religion, and join the congregation of CHRIST, we recede also from *the signs* of this religion, because our adopted religion ignores, and more, condemns them.

Crosses, charms, images, crucifixes, and other

superstitious heathen usages, in which the Gentiles delight, we leave to them, caring only, and striving only, with as little of symbolism as is consistent with order and propriety, "*in spirit and in truth,*" to serve God in the Gospel of His Son Jesus Christ, our Lord.

VII.

When, before, half in jest, it was said that Hector, Achilles, and their associates might ("in the tale of Troy divine") have possibly been seen in the hostile ranks airing themselves, like some modern Lydia, with Crosses round their necks, I was not aware that there existed evidence which makes the thing not only possible, but probable.

For, on the breast of a hero who might have flourished at an earlier period than those famous warriors (say B.C. 1200), we actually find a Cross portrayed. The hero is one of the "*Seven chiefs against Thebes,*" and his portrait with Cross thereon suspended is painted on an Etruscan alabaster vase, at Volterra in Italy.

Here the Cross is,

as given in " The Gentleman's Magazine" of 1863, p. 80.

IX.

But now, leaving awhile the Cross *Pagan,* let us come to the Cross *Christian.*

Distinguish, first, between the *Cross* and the *Crucifix.*

The Cross, as a sign of Christianity, did not come into public use in the Church till after the time of Constantine, who died A.D. 337, at which period superstition abounded. Dean Burgon (" Letters from Rome," 1862, p. 210) says, writing of the

Catacombs, " I question whether a Cross occurs in *any* Christian monument of the first four centuries."

In this case, the Cross is comparatively of modern application to Christ.

To the Dean I have subsequently written (1878), to ask him to be so obliging as to inform me if such be still his opinion. He has answered in the affirmative.

At the same date, I also wrote to Mr. Parker, C.B. (Keeper of the Ashmolean Museum, Oxford), the learned Roman antiquary, so well known by his antiquarian works, whose acquaintance I had the pleasure of making at Rome, to ask his mind on the subject.

He replied, that he thought the Dean perfectly correct in his opinion.

With two such authorities, this question, therefore, I presume, must be considered as settled.

As to the symbols of the Catacombs generally, implicit reliance is by no means to be placed on them, whether *in situ*, or in the Vatican Museum. They have been *restored*, embellished, and what not.

Pope Damasus, in the latter part of the fourth century, did much in this way. And Pope John, at the end of the sixth, carried on the same work. Hence, caution in drawing inferences is needed.

The *Crucifix*, or Cross with a figure attached to it

cruci-fix, did not appear in the Church till long after —say another 200 years.

In reference to the Crucifix, Zoeckler (p. 125) says:

" As regards the representation of the Saviour on the Cross, the earliest art of the Church imposed on itself the severest restraint. For, according to the distinct evidence of the monuments, *crucifix figures, whether painted or plastic,* in the two first centuries *after Constantine,* are *altogether wanting."* The italics are his.

Thus, according to this writer, it was not till 500 years after Christ, and over, that superstition and apostasy had sufficiently perverted the Christian Church, so as to lead men to the audacious act of forming a graven image of their God to worship.

"Thou shalt not make to thyself the likeness of anything in heaven above, or in the earth beneath.

" Thou shalt not bow down to them, nor worship them."

Where observe, that such things are by God's command not to be made as objects of religious worship, nor *to be bowed down to.*

X.

As to the *punishment of* CRUCIFIXION. This is very ancient. It prevailed in early ages of the world in Egypt, Persia, Assyria, India, Greece, Italy, Germany—perhaps everywhere. In Persia (in China, too, it is said) it exists up to the present time; for Captain Marsh, in his "Ride Through Islam," 1877, p. 104, saw *three men crucified on a wall* in "Meshid the holy." Their faces were towards the wall, and "large wooden tent-pegs were driven through their hands and feet, and one through the back."

Another Oriental punishment, of which crucifixion is a form, is *impalement,* which means being placed on a *palus* (Latin) or *pale* (whence *paling*), or stake.

This frightful torture seems to be of three kinds. One, just described. Another, where the sufferer is impaled on the sharpened stake passing under the skin *outside,* and along the whole length of, the backbone, the stake coming out at the shoulders. The other is, when the poor sufferer is made to *sit,* and is forcibly pressed down on the stake, which thus enters his intestines, piercing his vitals. " Acutâ si sedeam cruce "— If I should sit on the

sharp Cross, or stake. (From quotation in Se-
neca, given in Lipsius, "*De Cruce.*")

In these two cases the victim of this ferocious
crime is literally *spitted*. In one case the spit is
short, in the other long, and each *fixed* firmly into
the earth. "Sicut assos in verubus pisces"—as
fish spitted for roasting.

Again Lipsius, quoting Hesychius, also gives
a cut of the third torture, in which the cross
or stake, entering below, passes through the body,
and comes out at the mouth! It is so horrible that
I do not give it.

Which is the most cruel punishment—this or
crucifixion?

How fierce and alienated from God is the heart of
man which has devised and still perpetrates such
villainy!

They are the Serbs who are credited with the invention [wrongly?] of this crime, with which they visited
their prisoners when in the decline of the Roman
Empire they spread themselves over its provinces.
"They seem to have introduced impalement to the
notice of the Romans, as Procopius alludes to the
strange way of 'putting to death, not by spear
or sword, but planting in the earth sharp stakes,
upon which they placed these miserable creatures,
driving the sharp points of the stakes,' '*giù per le
parti pudende e spingendo drênto a gl' interiori, le*

tormentavano grandemente,' as Orbini, the early Slav historian, paraphrases it."—*Times* of Sept. 17, 1878.

In the British Museum we have specimens of the manner of impalement as practised by the Assyri-

ans. In the downstair (lowest) room, on Assyrian slabs are men *hanging on stakes* thrust into the body under the breastbone. Apparently they were prisoners taken in war. These may go back to B.C. about 700. This would be a fourth method.

Dr. Birch has kindly sent me from the British Museum a sketch of an impalement from the great bronze gates lately excavated in Assyria, and sent home. But it is too horrible to give here.

XI.

RETURN we, however, to the punishment of *Cruci-fixion.*

As to the shape of the Cross on which our blessed Lord suffered, it is impossible to speak with precision. It may have been in the form of the one we are in the habit of seeing—the Latin Cross. Not that we are to suppose it trim and polished, as the painters represent, but a *rough gibbet* such as was used for the vilest malefactors. Nor are we to suppose it *set on a hill,* for there was no hill thereabout to set it on. Neither (as the painters again mislead us) a *lofty structure,* but sufficiently low to admit the malefactor's legs to be broken (by a blow from the end of a spear, or a sword probably); yet, again sufficiently high not to admit of the sufferer's head, being reached by the hand of the spectators.

This is shown from the fact that to touch the lips of the Saviour with the moistened sponge, the pious hand had to be supplemented with a *cane* (probably the *arundo donax,* which grows everywhere on the Mediterranean), into the hollow of which the stalk of the hyssop, on which the sponge was placed, would, as I suppose, have been thrust. (Matt. xxvii.; John xix.)

In regard to the *quality* of the Cross above

alluded to, the writer in Smith's "Dictionary of the Bible," (article, "Cross") has these observations :

"It must not be overlooked that Crosses must have been of the *meanest and readiest materials*, because used in such marvellous numbers. Thus, Jannæus crucified 800 Jews per day; Varus, 2,000; Hadrian, 500; and Titus so many that there was not room for the crucified, nor Crosses wherewithal to crucify."

This incident reminds us of what happened in the case of the persecuted Waldenses in France, in the reign of Philip le Bel, 1302.

The mayor (I think of Toulouse) wrote to Paris for instruction as to what he was to do : "for," said he, "there are yet plenty of heretics at large, while the prisons are so full that they will contain no more, nor is there stone nor mortar to build."

The king in answer checked the persecutor's zeal. "We advise *delay as may be expedient.*"

The Cross was called *arbor*, or *lignum infelix*, the unhappy tree, as well it might.

So ignominious and hateful to the Romans was the punishment of the Cross, that Cicero says, "Not only let the Cross be absent from the person of Roman citizens, but *its very name* from their thoughts, eyes, and ears."

Crucifixion, we observed, was a species of *impale-ment*, the body being *outside* the stake, in other words attached to it. This attachment was effected either by cords or by nails.

Further, this instrument of torture would be *natural*, a tree growing; or *artificial*, a stake in-fixed in the earth.

This latter, again, would be *simple*, or *complex*. Simple, an upright trunk, or pole; complex, with limbs or adjuncts attached.

This brings us to *the Cross of our Lord*.

XII.

At once, we think of the Latin Cross with which we are all so familiar, the " *Crux immissa*," † and we have no doubt that it was on such a Cross that our blessed Lord was crucified. We seem to make sure of it.

But is not this one of the many things that with-out inquiring we take for granted " received by vain tradition from our fathers?"

Observe, I do not say that our Lord *was not* crucified on such a Cross; but I venture to suggest that it would be hard to *prove that He was*. How do we know that our Lord was not nailed to the *stauros*, the *upright stake without arms*, fixed into the earth, to which in its simple, stake-like shape so many were fastened, and died?

This was the simplest plan, the *most easy for the executioners*, and therefore most likely the one usually adopted. Our Lord's *might* have been an exception; but have we any reason for supposing that He was? Is it for a moment to be supposed that, generally, when executions took place by the thousand, the executioners were at the trouble of nailing cross-pieces (transoms) to the *stauros?*

The habit, then, would be the use of *the simple stake*. Besides, that mode while *giving less trouble* would make *less demand on the commissariat* for spike nails, or for rope, as the case might be.   .

The illustration on the next page is from the learned work of Professor Lipsius, *De Cruce*, p. 1159, Louvain, 1605.

It represents what he calls " *Crux simplex*," the most simple form of the Cross, a pole or stake, *the Stauros*, with a man nailed to it.

A Cross other than a mere stake he designates *genus compactum*, or *made up*. But both he calls *Crosses*.

There is, in fact, a difficulty about the term *Cross*. The following I take from Smith's Dictionary, article *Cross* :

" The word *Stauros* [the term used for *Cross* in the Greek Testament] properly means *merely a*

stake. In Livy, even, *Crux* means a *mere stake*. In consequence of this vagueness of meaning, *impaling* is sometimes spoken of loosely, as a *kind of crucifixion*.

"The Hebrews have no word for *Cross* more definite than '*wood*.' "

In reference further to the *form of the Cross* on which our Lord suffered, the writer of the article in question, Dr. Farrar, holds to its *traditionary shape,* that of the *Latin* Cross.   His assertion is strong, not so his reason.   Let the reader judge.   " That this was the kind of Cross on which our Lord died [says he] is obvious, among other reasons [he does not give them] from the mention of the ' title ' as placed above our Lord's head."

His only reason *given* for following " the almost unanimous tradition" (I quote his words) appears then to be, that were our Lord to have suffered on the ordinary *stauros* (the stake), there would have been no room for the " title" over His head.

Look, reader, at the above cut, and judge for yourselves of the force of the Canon's " reasons."

As for the tradition he speaks of, is this of much worth, think you ?

XIII.

THE form of the Cross adopted by the Eastern and Western churches, as we know, differs.

Which is most likely to be right ?

The Eastern follows, generally, the form of the pectoral of Samsi-Vul, the most ancient. The Western, that of the Cross of the gods Horus, Canopus, and Bacchus, with one limb lengthened, commonly called the *Latin Cross*, †.

This Cross in Western sacred symbolism has respect, not to the *person* but to the *passion* of Christ.

There is, however, another *quasi* Cross, which specially relates to the *person* of Christ, and it is this X (*Crux decussata*), or St. Andrew's Cross, the Greek letter *Ch*, which forms the beginning of the word CHRIST. It is exactly our X.

This is the most ancient, or earliest, of *Christian* signs, and was adopted by Constantine after his repeated vision, and by him placed on his standard, named " Labarum."

It is really *not a cross*, but the *letter* X (*ch*) the first letter of our Lord's title, " CH-rist."

We have then a Cross †, and a cross letter X, one referring to the *suffering*, the other to the *person* of the Lord Jesus, and the latter more ancient than the former. The former, however, has eclipsed the latter. The latter became, and remains to this day, almost obsolete. The Cross, the sign of the *passion* present in the hand, has eclipsed the *Person* of Christ absent, and *the mere physical act of the crucifixion overshadows* in the minds of millions upon millions the rest of Christ's work for us sinful men, now in course of accomplishment.

Reader, mark this well. See also how it is with yourself. Remember, too, that the Cross is only a *part, a small part,* of His suffering, and that His suffering is only *one part* (a great part, indeed), of what He *has* done, *is* doing, and yet *has to do,* for His Church.

Christendom in pictorial art (and Christendom, knowing little of the Bible, is mainly directed by pictorial art) sees and knows little of Christ, except as a *baby,* or as a *sufferer* on the tree. Artists present to her view, mainly, these two subjects, and beyond these, of the *Work* and *Person* of the Redeemer, she has but few ideas.

The art and device of man is, however, but a poor substitute for the Word of God.

Art, usually, is an enemy to the Word.

XIV.

We are now prepared to see how easily the Heathen, in adopting a nominal Christianity, as they

extensively did in the reign of Constantine, would
have modified and Christianised their views of the
Heathen Cross.

Hitherto that emblem had been *associated with
their worship of the gods*. In their temples, in their
houses, on their images, etc., the worshippers were
accustomed to see the peculiar Cross, or Crosses,
dedicated to each. Bacchus had his, Serapis his,
and so forth. Many of the new converts were
themselves in different instances wearing on their
own persons the emblem of their gods. To enter,
then, into a heathen temple just re-dedicated to
Christ, where the Cross of the rejected pagan deity
still existed, or where a new Christian Cross had
been just substituted—to visit a temple so reconse-
crated, or to enter a basilica, by the Emperor's order
just handed over to the bishop for Christian use—
all this would aid in making the change from the
worship *of the gods* to the worship of the *Emperor's
God* very easy to the convert.

The old temples, and the old basilicas, the arrangement of the apse, etc., in the latter almost unchanged
—the lustral, or holy, water—the mural paintings
sometimes left, sometimes altered to suit the worship of the new heroes or *saints*—the incense, the
pomp of worship, the long train of vested priests—
all, and much more, would make the transition from
the old to the new faith a matter of little difficulty.

As to the Cross, there it was, and there it would continue, and has continued to be.

And there for the present we leave it.

(For the above account of symbolism see article "Cross," in "*Dictionary of Church Antiquities*," London, 1875.)

XV.

THE following notice respecting the Cross gives a good idea of popular notions on the subject. It appeared in the *Church Times*, early in 1878, and is in form of an answer from one of the authorities of the paper to an inquiry. This pamphlet being merely a "fragment," I have left the thing as it first appeared.

"B. J. W.—The lecturer is so far right that the Greek word *stauros* does mean a pole, stake, or palisade, and no more, in early classical writings.

"But it is matter of plain history that the Romans used cross-beams, and not mere poles, for executing

criminals by nailing them hand and foot, and that
Josephus, and other later Greek writers, use *stauros*
to translate *crux*. And the evidence as to what the
early Christians believed to be the instrument of
the Passion is abundant and indisputable. The
shape varies between an X, a T, and a +, but never
consists of an upright only. *It is a Cross*, not a
pole, which Constantine the Great, the first Christian
Emperor, *adopted as his standard*. It is a Cross
which appears even earlier in the Catacombs, and
even in a very curious Pagan caricature lately discovered there, a Christian is depicted worshipping
an ass-headed figure fastened to a cross. It is a
cross which the emperors who succeeded Constantine, beginning with Valentinian I. in A.D. 364,
stamped on their coins, at the time when there were
thousands of people still living who remembered
the use of the cross as an instrument of death.
And whereas no such ambiguity exists in the Latin
word *crux* as in the Greek *stauros* (for *crux* means a
cross, and nothing else), this very word is used by
Tertullian, who died very old, about A.D. 240, three
hundred years before there were any Latin monks to
speak of, and also by St. Cyprian, who was mar-
tyred in 258.

" The doctor had better go to school, instead of
keeping one, if he exhibits so much ignorance."

The writer of the above sends the lecturer to school for his ignorance.

He in his reply to "B. J. W." needs some schooling himself, surely.

An exemplification of this need is the ungrounded assertion that *"crux* means a cross, *and nothing else;"* for we have already quoted Canon Farrar as making a directly contrary assertion. " In *Livy,*" says he, " crux means *a mere stake;"* and the Canon, in reference to *crux*, speaks further of its " *vagueness of meaning.*"

Next, as to the term *stauros* (Greek) being correctly translated *crux*, or cross, this nobody denies. But, to state, or to imply, that the Romans in crucifixion did not use *the stake* (*stauros*) simply, without the *transom* (or cross-beam), is to assert what it would be impossible to prove. (See cut from Lipsius' *De Cruce* above.)

No one, of course, denies that the Romans used in executions the *stauros* with *transom*—in other words, the cross proper; but did they not also use the *stauros*, or stake, by itself ? Who will prove the contrary ?

XVI.

THAT, as the *Church Times'* writer says, the early Christians believed that our Lord was hung on a transverse beam, one does not deny. Their traditional testimony, however, is not *proof.* At the same time, on well thinking over the matter, I am inclined to come to this conclusion, and am also moved to this by the "graffito blasfemo" — the *blasphemous caricature,* above alluded to.

This *scribble*—a mere scratch it is—was found

November, 1857; not, as our critic says, in the Catacombs at Rome, but in a very different locality, namely, *in the palace of the Cæsars,* on the Palatine Hill.

4—2

The workmen, at the above date, were excavating there, as for years past they have been, and came to this curious scratch on the wall. It represents in *the rudest manner* a crucifixion, the arms extended on a cross. The figure is human, with the head of a beast, but *not of an ass*, as given in the passage above, the ears being *remarkably small*.

The Padre Garrucci, an antiquarian, thinks it is that of a *wild ass*, "*onagre.*" I differ.

Father Garrucci describes it, and is quoted by Canon Liddon in his seventh Bampton Lecture, p. 593. Father Garrucci gives interesting particulars, and attributes the date to the very early part of the third century. Whether in this he be correct or not, I do not pretend to say.

The Canon falls, I observe, into the usual error of the " *ass's* head."

This strange *Crucifix* in the caricature does not stand alone. There is on its right side a figure in mean attire, which seems to be engaged in worship. To this an ill-spelt legend, rudely scratched beneath in Greek characters, agrees, for it is to this effect: " ALEXAMENOS WORSHIPS HIS GOD."

It was probably the work of some illiterate slave, or soldier, attached to the palace of the Cæsars, ridiculing the religion of a companion.

A facsimile (photograph) of the *Graffito sacro* is, as I write, before me. The original, I was told, was in the Kircher (magic-lantern inventor) Museum in the former vast Jesuit College at Rome, of which he was a member. So I went there to look for it.

It is not easy to find, being a small thing in a small room (a scribe sits in it), at the top of the building. It is on the left of the entrance corridor, and on the left side of said little room, suspended close to a window.

It is so insignificant, that one might very easily overlook it. My photo is seven inches by six. The original is somewhat larger, a mass of scratches and disfigurements, so that the *engravings* of the originals which you see give very little idea of its indistinctness. He was a sharp fellow who discovered it.

But, *there it is* clear enough, when you know where to look for it, showing the practised eye of him who first detected it.

The substance on which the scratch is made (for *scratch* is the word which best describes the thing) is fine white stucco—the fineness of the polished material, soiled as it is, being in great contrast to the rude effort of the coarse hand of the untaught limner—so untaught, that to discuss the beast's head he intended to represent is superfluous. I should not wonder if it were intended for a *Jackal* —the Egyptian *Anubis*.

XVII.

As to the *Church Times'* assertion of the Cross appearing *earlier* than the time of CONSTANTINE, it is unfounded. There may be Crosses in catacombs, but superstition has sometimes, *at a later date*, supplied them. The authorities before quoted, Dean Burgon and Mr. Parker, on this head are sufficient.

The next error we notice is contained in this sentence : "It is *a Cross*, not a pole, which Constantine the Great, the first Christian Emperor, adopted as his standard."

This would lead one to believe that it was a Cross so, †, or perhaps so, ✕, that the Emperor (a painful mixture of Heathenism and Christianity) magnified.

Not at all. *It was no Cross, but two letters*, which Constantine introduced, the Greek letter *Chi* joined with another Greek letter, *Ro*, which united thus form a *monogram ;*

which reads in English CHR, the *first three letters of the title* CHRIST. In Greek the *Chi* is exactly our X, and the *Ro* our P.

It was not, then, a Cross, but *two letters* which the Emperor adopted and placed upon his banners, and not on his banners only, but on his armour, and on that of his soldiers.

BARONIUS, the Cardinal, and annalist of the Roman Church (died A.D. 1607), who from the first of Christianity gives the annals of Emperors and Popes, adds also to his great work some of their coins and medals. From some of those of the earlier *Christian* emperors, it is proposed now to illustrate the progress of the use of the Cross in the early Christian Church, and the consequent decline of the monogram CHR.

The Emperors are both of the Eastern and Western Empires.

But let this be premised, that if the Cross was now about to be introduced into the Christian Church, it was both to *Christians and Pagans alike an old familiar, sacred, sign bound up with the earliest recollections of childhood, and universally connected with the worship of the gods.* Every race of mankind in some form or other was familiar with the Cross. So great was their number, that the writer of an admirable article in the *Edinburgh Review* of October, 1870, on " The Pre-Christian Cross," informs us that he has collected nearly 200 varieties of its Heathen form.

XVIII.

As to the antiquity and universality of the use of the Cross, the following is the testimony of the same learned writer:

"From the dawn of organised Paganism in the Eastern world to the final establishment of Christianity in the Western, *the Cross* was undoubtedly *the commonest and most sacred* of symbolical monuments, and to a remarkable extent *it is so still* in almost every land where that of Calvary is unrecognised or unknown. Apart from any distinctions of social or intellectual superiority of caste, colour, nationality, or location, in either hemisphere it appears to have been the aboriginal possession of every people of antiquity—the elastic girdle, so to say, which embraced the most widely separated heathen communities, the most significant token of an universal brotherhood, the principal point of contact in every system of Pagan mythology, to which *all the families of mankind* were severally and irresistibly drawn, and by which their common descent was emphatically expressed" (p. 224).

And again: "Of the several varieties of the Cross still in vogue as national or ecclesiastical emblems in this and other European states, and

distinguished by the familiar appellations of St.
George, St. Andrew, the Maltese, the Greek, the
Latin, etc., etc., *there is not one amongst them* the
existence of which may not be traced to the remotest antiquity" (p. 226).

We proceed now, from the monuments (coins and
medals) preserved by BARONIUS, a most devoted
Papist, and so, on such subjects, an unobjectionable
authority, to show how the *Chi-Ro* which, as the
Monogram of Christ, represented His *Person*, was
gradually in the Church *pushed out of use* by the
Cross, which was the symbol *only of His Passion*,
in common use, moreover, in the worship of the
"gods many" of the Heathen.

The *Chi-Ro* and the Cross are both, be it remembered, mere *humanly-invented* symbols, *both alike
unrecognised in Scripture*. The former of these,
however, is the more ancient in the Christian Church.

In his work on the Catacombs (London, 1847),
Dr. C. Maitland observes, in reference to the adoption of the cross in place of the *Chi-Ro :*

" In undergoing this change its original intention
was lost. From being a token of joy, an object to
be crowned with flowers [he gives an illustration
of the *Chi-Ro* so crowned], a sign in which to con-
quer—it became a *thing of agony and tears*—a

stock-subject with the artist anxious to display his power of representing *anguish*" (p. 202).

The same writer, speaking of the small Byzantine museum at the Vatican, adds, p. 205 : "Every subject from the treatment of the artist becomes more or less *distressing*. 'The Man of Sorrows,' covered with triangular splashes of blood, with a face indicative of hopeless anguish, illustrates less the Redeemer's life, than *a dark page in the history of Christendom*. The last glimmering of Divine Majesty suffered total eclipse from the *exclusive display of agonised humanity*."

Even so. Christ *in His humiliation*, as a sufferer, or as a helpless infant, is, I had almost said, alone presented in pictorial art. In His glory, as the brother and risen head of our glorified humanity —"Behold, I and the children whom Thou hast given Me"—He is hardly known.

As to the "*triangular splashes* of blood" above-mentioned, at Rome, they have (1878) introduced in this way something new. On their gaudily-painted — say, intensely-painted—crucifixes, they have, on the body and limbs of the image of the Crucified One, introduced great and frequent blood-gouts *in relief* of *blood colour* shocking to behold.

How sensuous must be that religion which, like that of heathenism, requires such stimulants to devotion ! "Faith cometh by *hearing*," *not* by seeing.

XIX.

But to return to our subject.

Comparing the relative value of the two signs, it is, I think, M. Didron, the great French iconographist, who says : " The *Monogram,* which on the banner of Constantine expressed the name of CHRIST, published much more openly to the world the triumph of Christianity than did the idea of the Cross."

Naturally, and necessarily. Most just is his observation.

The Monogram was, so to speak, *Christ in Person,* as before observed. Besides, it was a new sign to the Heathen of a new religion. The other, old and familiar, presented to them nothing new—certainly nothing *heavenly,* but stank of their pristine Paganism, naturalised in the temples of their gods.

But this Cross—*this universal symbol*—whence came it ? What means it ?

Who can tell! Old as the earliest age of civilisation, one cannot speak decisively either as to its origin or design, though some say otherwise.

As to its *design,* MAURICE, in his *Indian Antiquities* (1793, part iii. p. 387), has perhaps given the best solution. He considers it as "*the emblem*

of universal nature, of that earth, to the four quarters of which its diverging radii pointed."
Such is the idea of this learned author, and I doubt if any other solution of the mysterious emblem, equally satisfactory, has been given.

Of CONSTANTINE it is thus that Niebuhr, *Rom. Hist.,* vol. iii. p. 303, writes :

" His motives in establishing the Christian religion are something very strange, indeed. The religion there was in his head must have been a mere jumble. On his coins he has ' *The unconquered sun.*' He worships pagan deities; consults the soothsayers; holds heathen superstitions. Yet, he shuts up the temples, and builds churches.

" As president of the Nicene Council, we can only look on him with disgust. He was himself no Christian at all, and would only be baptised when in the article of death. He had taken up the Christian faith as a superstition, which he mingled with all his other superstitions. To call him even a saint is a profanation of the word.

" In other respects Constantine was not a bad man; yet the death of his son Crispus must be deemed a shocking event."

He put to death also his brother-in-law, Licinius, another " shocking event."

XX.

LET us now trace, from the annals of CARDINAL BARONIUS, the progress of the Cross in the Christian Church, and mark how this Heathen emblem gradually and successfully ejected in public and private

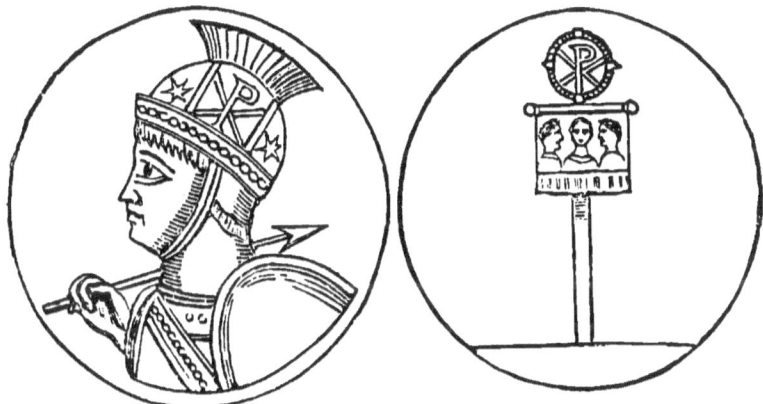

Fig. 1. CONSTANTINE with *Chi-Ro* on his helmet.   Fig. 2. His Banner with *Chi-Ro.*

the earlier, better, and Christian symbol, the letters *Chi-Ro*, the MONOGRAM OF CHRIST.

Fig. 1. CONSTANTINE it was, as we have seen, who first *published abroad* the Monogram.   And this he did on the armour of his soldiers, on his own, and, notably, on his *military standard* called the *Labarum*.

CONSTANTINE, his vision, his conversion, all three are unsatisfactory.

Here he is as represented on one of his coins given by Baronius (Fig. 1). On his helmet you observe the *Chi-Ro*.

Of Constantines there were several. This one is commonly called "*The Great*," and was son of Constantius. He held the Roman Empire thirty years, built Constantinople, and died A.D. 337.

The following is from Zœcler's "Cross of Christ," p. 145:

"The coins of Constantine display to a great extent Heathen emblems. Their impressions frequently figure *Apollo* with the sun-ball, sometimes also *Mars, Victory,* or the *Genius of the Roman people,* whilst others appear adorned with the monogram of the *Christian's God.* They reflect the strange Christo-heathen medley of religion which remained peculiar to his whole policy of government, a policy conditionated by his twofold position as *Protector of the Church* on the one hand, and Roman *Pontifex Maximus* on the other.

"One of his coins, with the reverse inscribed 'to the Sun, the (or my) unconquered companion,' '*Soli invicto Comiti,*' places an equal-armed, or Greek cross, immediately beside the figure of the *Sun-god.* And, even at the consecration of Constantinople as his Christian residence, a solemn procession was held, in which the statue of the Emperor, holding in its right hand a *Goddess of Fortune,* whose head was adorned with a cross, was enthroned in place of the Sun in the chariot of that divinity."

Fig. 2. Observe next his standard, the famous *Labarum*. It is from a medal, is made (they say) of *silk*, and the curious heads on it inwrought represent the Emperor, and some of his family.

The *material*, I should rather suppose, would have been of the same kind of stuff—a thick brocade—of which that curious piece of antiquity is formed, preserved in the Church of St. Martino in Monte, at Rome, *the mitre of St. Sylvester*, contemporary with Constantine. This also, like the veil of the Labarum, is "inwrought with figures dim."

See it, reader, if you can; and may you find in the church the same courteous monk who showed the relic to me.

If that relic be authentic, and it may be so, I cannot but think in looking on it you see the same kind of stuff that Constantine's banner was made of.

The *fringe* of the Labarum also observe, and, not least, the *Chi-Ro*, crowning all, encircled with a jewelled coronet.

Fig. 3. Another form of the same we here have, a little varied. The standard with the *Chi-Ro* differently placed also belongs to Constantime.

XXI.

Fig. 4. We come now to Constantius the Second He retains the *Chi-Ro,* but introduces the Cross.

Julian (called the Apostate), his successor, who reigns under two years, rejects as a heathen, both the *Chi-Ro* and the *Cross,* and re-introduces on his

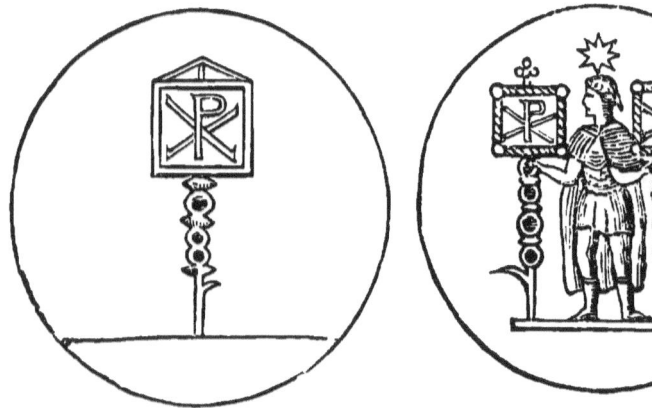

Fig. 3. Constantine's Banner   Fig. 4. Constantius II.: Banner
     with *Chi-Ro.*   with Cross *added* to the *Chi-Ro.*

standards the old " S. P. Q. R."—*Senate and Roman People.*

Fig. 5. Jovian reigned seven months (d. a.d. 364). His standard is the *Chi-Ro* with Cross above. Below are two captives (a Heathen glorification) chained.

Fig. 6. Valens (East, d. a.d. 378). On his standard *the Cross is first found alone.* The Heathen Victory marks the style of his Christianity.

VALENS was killed near Adrianople in the great victory there gained over the Emperor by the Goths.

"The fatal consequences of this battle," says Gibbon, "far surpassed the misfortune which Rome

Fig. 5. Jovian, Chi-Ro *and* Cross.   Fig. 6. Valens : *Chi-Ro* excluded Cross and goddess Victoria.

sustained in the field of Cannæ. The slaughter was equal."

Fig. 7. VALENTINIAN (West), brother of Valens, reigned eleven years (d. A.D. 375). He is represented with a sceptre in the form of *a double Cross* on a globe.

Fig. 8. THEODOSIUS I. (d. 395). He has a *jewelled Cross for a sceptre.* In his reign, which lasted sixteen years, the use of the Cross becomes common, and the *Chi-Ro,* proportionably disappears. Two large Latin crosses—one jewelled—are seen in this reign

5

on the tomb of a certain PROBUS. (*Baronius,* vol. vii. p. 245).

Fig. 7. Valentinian.　　　　Fig. 8. Theodosius.

Fig. 9. EUDOXIA, empress (d. 460), *wears a Cross on her head.*

Her head with the Cross. How strongly in this she resembles the heathen Diana before rendered! This is that Eudoxia who sent *St. Peter's chains* from Jerusalem to Rome, where they built for them the *Basilica Eudoxiana.* There I saw them in 1877 being furbished up for a fête.

Fig. 10. The same EUDOXIA, wife of Theodosius II., just figured with a Cross *on her head.* Here she holds *one in each hand.* She was a Greek of great abilities, daughter of the philosopher Leontius. She was ambitious, aspiring, vindictive, was divorced, and died in exile. (*Gibbon,* c. xvi.)

She, observe, has adopted the *nimbus* or circle of glory. This is again an evidence of the Heathenising of the Church. For the *nimbus* belongs then, and now, to Heathendom. *M. Didron* tells us that for the three first centuries the Church utterly rejected it, as Heathenish.

9. Eudoxia.   10. Eudoxia.

Fig. 11. HONORIA, sister of *Valentinian*, daughter of *Placidia*, was of loose character; and for a traitorous intrigue with Attila, king of the Huns, to whom she made love, " was immured in a perpetual prison," where she died some time after, A.D. 450. (*Gibbon*, c. xvii.)

The Cross on the shoulder ; how different from the Cross on the heart!

Fig. 12. PULCHERIA (d. 454), daughter of *Arcadius*, and Empress of the East, of great talents for government; a *saint* also, her title to that dignity being

5—2

manifested—according to the debased religion of the age—by her leading a life of celibacy, though a married woman! This was *before marriage* stipulated for by her. Such are *Rome's* saints, not God's!

11. Honoria.　　　　　　12. Pulcheria.

Her Cross is nearly identical with that of SAMSI-VUL.

"*Quam in postica vides Crucem coronâ cinctum, eam super diadema gestare consuevisse Christianas Imperatrices, quæ sunt dicta superius satis docent*"—which means, What I have before said, that the Cross on the other side (the coin) is that which the empresses were in the habit of wearing above the diadem, shews.—BARONIUS *in loco*. The diadem (a fillet for the head) was the emblem of empire.

The originals of the above figures are taken from

the numerous and ponderous folios—twenty-nine of them—of Baronius (Ed. *Lucæ*, 1741). He tells us that they are from coins and medals (often in gold), and gives the names of the *virtuosi* to whom in his day they belonged. They are executed in the coarsest style.

Zeno (d. 491), as with kings in modern times, carries the orb *surmounted with the Cross.*

The illustration below (from *Dictionary of Christian Antiquities*) is of the Cross worn on the head *by a man*—and that man the wretched murderer, usurper, and tyrant, Phocas (d. 610).

Phocas.

XXII.

THUS the *Chi-Ro* went out, and the Cross came in. The Monogram of CHRIST disappeared, and a Heathen emblem took its place. The emblem will illustrate the debased Christianity of the times.

The common assertion that CONSTANTINE adopted the Cross as his standard has thus been disproved. They were *letters*, not a Cross, he adopted, whatever value may be attached to the fact.

"Stranger"—as the Americans after the Greeks well say—"Stranger," you remember his column in the *Forum*, at Rome—that column, which in Byron's day was,

"Thou, nameless column, with a buried base."

It was in 1816 that the *buried base* was laid bare, and the odious name, PHOCAS, discovered on it.

PHOCAS, the friend of the Papacy, who, by his famous decree (604) in that dark age constituted the Pope of Rome *Universal Bishop*, who gave him the Pantheon, "which hitherto consecrated to *Cybele and all the gods*, was now dedicated, characteristically, to *Mary* (the Cybele of the Roman system) and to *all the martyrs*"—*gods* of Papal Rome. (*Elliott's Horæ*, vol. iii., p. 277).

He wears the Cross (on his helmet), so also on his

helmet does HERACLIUS, who dethroned and destroyed
him. It was the fashion of the day, the Pagan sign
proclaiming the Pagan Christianity of the age passed
into debased superstition. What did not the martial
HERACLIUS himself do! Having recovered in war
from the King of Persia, CHOSROES, what passed as
the "*true Cross*," he carried it into Jerusalem on
his shoulder! Had he lived a thousand years later,
he would have taken off his shoes, and flat on his
stomach have adored the Cross, as PIO NONO on the
floor of the Sistine.

There is in the old church at Dieppe on the N.
side, a painted window giving the Emperor carrying
the Cross.

This *material* kind of religion is just the Heathenism which belongs to us all, rulers, priests, warriors,
plebs., until the WORD OF GOD and THE SPIRIT OF
GOD have taught us *Christianity*.

XXIII.

WITH Crosses, these adopted Pagan emblems, *Christianity* has nothing to do.

We have adverted to the fact that the forms of nearly 200 Heathen crosses had been collected by an individual.

Subjoined are some of great antiquity—probably over 1000 years before Christ—lately discovered in

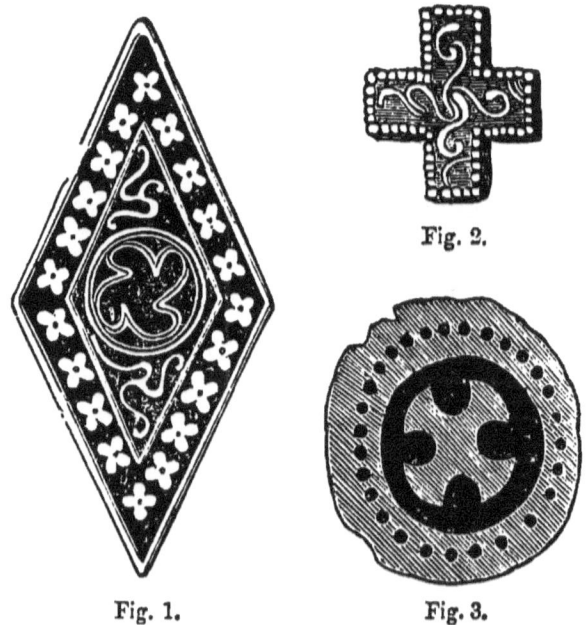

Fig. 2.

Fig. 1.   Fig. 3.

Greece, at Mycenæ, by Dr. SCHLIEMANN, in the supposed tomb of *Agamemnon*, the leader of the expedition against Troy.

No. 1, a lozenge-shaped ornament, is of wood

covered with gold repoussée work; the centre, however, in intaglio. At the several corners are pairs of knobs, which, as the *Crosses* on it are our alone object, are omitted. These Crosses are of a common shape, and the same as those lately discovered by Captain Burton, near Bologna (*Etruscan Bologna*, 1877), on some pre-Christian pottery, and figured by him.

No. 2 is also *in gold*, little varying, it may be observed, from the one before figured, and represented as being worn by one of the heroes engaged against Thebes, not far from the æra of Agamemnon, so that one sees the *style of Cross in fashion* in those early days.

And how entirely one with the Cross now in use!

No. 3 is *in pottery*. We recognise in it a form nearly approaching that of our friend Samsi-Vul.

XXIV.

But of the Crosses the most notable is the one in *the form of the Greek* T (*Tau*), which slightly altered at top now forms the modern Latin Cross.

Here it is in two forms.

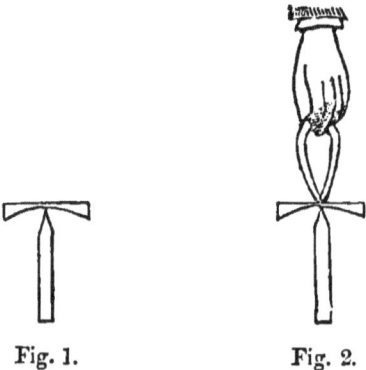

Fig. 1.   Fig. 2.

1, without a handle.

2, with a handle (the *crux ansata*). With the Egyptians it was "*the sign of life.*"

Its origin no one knows. Its use is universal in India and in Egypt, where in the monuments of each country it is held in the hands of the gods. It is also a charm of power.

In the latter country, whether they ever used the *Chi-Ro* I do not know; but the Tau was there *adopted* from early times by the Christians, and at the same period was being commonly used both by the followers of *Isis* and of *Jesus*.

On this subject Sir Gardner Wilkinson, in his
"*Ancient Egyptians*" (vol. i. p. 277), thus remarks :

"This curious fact is connected with the *Tau* in
later times, that the early Christians of Egypt
adopted it in lieu of the Cross, which (Cross) was
afterwards substituted for it [*i.e.,* took its place].
They prefixed it [the *Tau*] to inscriptions in the
same manner as the Cross in later times. Numerous inscriptions headed by the *Tau* are preserved
to the present day in early Christian sepulchres in
the Great Oasis."

A remarkable testimony !

Observe what follows :

"The adoption of this Heathen emblem was probably *a compromise,* a sort of equivocation in which,
whilst *they,* the Christians, saw a memento of the
Passion of Christ, *their Heathen* enemies, or friends,
as the case might be, *saw only the emblem of the
gods.* "The Christian adoption of pre-Christian
Crosses is supposed by Martini (a learned Jesuit,
1651) and others, to be what he calls *formes dis-
simulées* [dissembled forms], or ancient symbols
adopted by Christians as *sufficiently like the cross,* or
tree of punishment, to convey to their minds the
associations of our Lord's sufferings without proclaiming it in a manner which would *shock Heathen
prejudices* unnecessarily" (*Dict. of Christian Antiquities,* p. 495).

You blame them, reader?—" Of course I do."
You do well; but wait till you are similarly tried.

XXV.

In regard to the early use of the Cross, "As in
the oldest temples and catacombs of ancient Egypt,
so this type (the *Tau*) likewise abounds in the
ruined cities of Mexico and Central America, graven
as well upon the most ancient cyclopean and poly-
gonal walls, as upon the more modern and perfect
examples of masonry.   It is displayed in an equally
conspicuous manner upon the breasts of innume-
rable bronze statues which have been recently dis-
interred from the cemetery of Juigalpa (of unknown
antiquity) in Nicaragua." (*The Pre-Christian Cross*,
p. 230 ; *Edinburgh Review*, January, 1870.)

   " It was also distinguished by the [R.C.] Catholic
appellations, ' the *tree of subsistence*,' ' *the wood of
health*,' '*the emblem of life*.'   The last-mentioned
title was that by which it was called popularly in
Egypt, and by which the *suastika*, fire-machine, or
holy **Tau**, of the Buddhists, is now known.

" In South America (as above intimated) it was believed to be endued with power to restrain evil spirits" (p. 233, *Ibid*).

"Why," said I, one day at Naples to the coachman of a friend beside whom I was sitting on the box—"Why," said I, with a view of eliciting what he thought, " is that Cross placed there ?" pointing to one on a house we were passing.

His immediate reply was, " *To keep off evil spirits.*" Thus spoke *the natural man !*

Whether in Pagan Mexico, or Papal Italy, the religion of the material Cross is alike *the religion of nature.*

"To the close of the Middle Ages the stole, or *Isian* mantle, of the Cistercian monk was usually adorned with the ' croix patée,' cruciform hammer, and *nuns* wore it suspended from their necklaces, precisely in the same manner as did the *Vestal Virgins of Pagan Rome*" (p. 239).

" It may be seen on the bells of many of our parish churches, placed there as a *magic sign to subdue* the vicious spirit of the *tempest*" (p. 239).

The above are quotations from *The Pre-Christian Cross, Edinburgh Review.*

" It is a fact," says MAURICE (*Indian Antiquities,* quoted also by the Reviewer), " not less remarkable than well attested, that the Druids in their groves were accustomed to select the most stately and beautiful tree as an emblem of the deity they adored, and, having cut off the side branches, they affixed two of the largest of them to the highest part of the trunk in such a manner that those branches extended on each side like the arms of a man, and together with the body presented the appearance of a huge cross. On the bark in several places was also inscribed the *letter Tau*" (p. 242).

He then quotes Mr. King (*The Gnostics and their Gems*), who, speaking of the *tree-tau* being found on the famous image of *Serapis* when destroyed at Alexandria, says, "This Cross seems to be the Egyptian *Tau*, that ancient symbol of the generative power, and therefore transposed into the *Bacchic mysteries*. Such a Cross is found on the wall of a house at Pompeii in juxtaposition with such a symbol, both symbols embodying the same idea" (p. 242).

XXVI.

The *Tau* is also taken by some as representing *Tammuz* (*Adonis*, or possibly *Bacchus*) as being the first letter of his name. He is probably the *sun personified,* each year dying, and living — six months (so runs the myth) with Proserpine, and six months with Venus.

"Women weeping for Tammuz" (Ezek. viii.). Him Milton (always abounding in classic lore) grandly, thus :

> "Tammuz came next behind,
> Whose annual wound in Lebanon allured
> The Syrian damsels to lament his fate
> In amorous ditties, all a summer day,
> While smooth Adonis from his native rock
> Ran purple to the sea supposed with blood
> Of Tammuz, yearly wounded. The love tale
> Infected Zion's daughters with like heat,
> Whose wanton passions in the sacred porch,
> Ezekiel saw."
>
> *Paradise Lost,* b. i. 446.

"*Supposed with blood.*" The fable originated, no doubt, in the fact that when the snows of Lebanon melt and the river is in flood, a quantity of *red earth* is reached by the stream, whereby it becomes discoloured—as is often elsewhere seen. Hence the fiction from the fact.

MAUNDREL saw the stream "run purple to the sea." Less fortunate, in crossing it in May, 1872, I saw it in its natural state. Yet more fortunate in this respect, I am able to testify to the goodness and beauty of the trout which haunt this and the other "streams from Lebanon."

The scene of this fact and fable are only a few hours' ride along the shore north of Beyrout, and near to the place of another like myth—that of

St. George and the Dragon. Gibbon tells us that "this infamous George of Cappadocia, was bacon-factor to the army, who accumulated wealth by the basest arts of fraud." He became Archbishop of Alexandria—was polluted by cruelty and avarice—and was, A.D. 361, torn in pieces by the people, "and has been transformed into the renowned St. George of England" (ch. xxiii.).

What shall we say to *St. George's Cross?*

To return a moment to the supposed *Tau* of Tammuz, Adonis, or Bacchus.

To his worship, at the *mouth* of the stream Adonis, the town *Byblus* was devoted, whilst at its remote and sequestered *source* in Lebanon, *Venus*, with rites obscene, was honoured, rites so vile that CON-STANTINE ordered her temple to be destroyed, as being a pollution to the earth.

Here, if not the *Tau*, the Bacchic Cross would have been present, a witness, and aid to the pollu-tion. (See *Handbook for Syria.* "BYBLUS.")

XXVII.

In devotion, in reference to the use of material representations, such as crosses, and others similar, Bishop Andrews (?) has well observed :

"It cannot be doubted such gross illustrations are calculated rather to *prevent*, than excite, religious apprehension. And, as no worship but such as is spiritual can be acceptable to God, such things are rather *hindrances* than helps to devotion. St. Augustin says : '' They *deserve to err*, who will seek Christ not in inspired books, but on painted walls.'

"In the folly of the crucifix they easily bring Christ into contempt. In the crucifix they show that Christ suffered *no more than the crucifix* shows [represents]. But Christ suffered in soul the pains of hell, which no painter in the world is able to paint.

"They say," adds Bishop Andrews, "they will show His shape as He was in the days of His flesh.

"We answer, that as they be teachers of lies, so this image [the crucifix] teaches us to *forget* by it. For the whole Church hath taught us, that Christ suffered *more than we can see painted*. The especial pains and torments that He suffered for our sins are forgotten—the heavy wrath of His Father poured out in most full manner upon Him. So,

6

consequently, the image [crucifix] hath taught us *to forget the greatest part* of His passion.

"The makers and worshippers of images pretend to help us by pictures presented to the eye of the body. But it is not the eye of sense, but *the eye of faith*, that can give us true notions and right conceptions of this subject.

"Men can paint the cursed tree, but not the curse of the law that made it. Men can paint Christ bearing the Cross to Calvary, but not Christ ' bearing the sins of many.' We can describe the nails piercing the sacred flesh; but who can describe eternal justice piercing both flesh and spirit! We may describe the soldier's spear, but not the arrows of the Almighty; the cup of vinegar which He had tasted, but not the cup of wrath which He drank to the lowest dregs; the derision of the Jews, but not the desertion of the Almighty, forsaking His Son that He might never forsake us."

XXVIII.

The Cross worshipped by Pio Nono lying flat on his stomach, I observed I had seen (with many others) in the Sistine Chapel at Rome.

The worship of THE CRUCIFIX by the people at Rome is thus exemplified.

"In the temple of Hercules at Agrigentum, in Sicily, there is, says Cicero in his oration against Verres (4, § 43), a bronze statue of the god. Its mouth and chin are a little worn away, because the people in their prayers and thanksgivings not only worship, but kiss it."

I cannot give you a sketch of this Hercules; but read what follows and look at the sketch below.

BRAZEN CRUCIFIX in the Mamertine prison at Rome (Church of St. Joseph), the face entirely worn away by the kisses of the people.

"In the temple of Joseph, at Rome in Italy, there is a brazen statue of Jesus. Its mouth and chin are

6—2

much worn away, because people in their prayers
and thanksgivings not only worship, but kiss it."
(Roman *Guide Book*.)

Hercules and Jesus! Both imaged in brass—both
images "worshipped" with "prayers and thanksgivings," both doted on by the people, both kissed
by them—both so kissed that the solid brass is worn
away, and in the image of the latter still more than
in that of the former.

A curious parallel this, and one more exact between Heathen and Christian idolatry it would be
difficult to find.

I have known this crucifix for many years, and
usually when at Rome visit it, offensive as the den is
in the vestibule of which it is placed.

"Let the men who worship kiss the calves," it
was said in old time in Syria.

"Let the men who worship kiss the beard of
Hercules," it was said in Sicily.

"Let the men who worship kiss the crucifix," it
is now said to men in Rome.

Apis, Hercules, the Crucifix, all idols!

Wherein does the modern differ from the ancient
idolatry?

XXIX.

HERE, again, is Venus, and the Cross in the familiar "orb and cross." Reverse the book, and see.

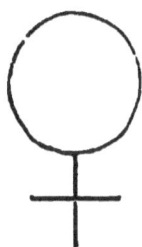

"The imperial globe is a globe terrestrial crowned by a Cross, being the significant *Christian* counterpart of the ancient oriental (*Heathen*) symbol of the mirror of Venus, or handled cross (*crux ansata*), of which it would appear to be a simple reversal (turned upside down). We first meet with it upon the coins of the Emperors Valentinian and Gratian." (*Zoeckler*, p. 156.)

"Only after Justinian (A.D. 565), does the cross-surmounted ball become gradually the prevalent mode of presentment, according to which *the Labarum is seen to be entirely replaced by the later symbol of the imperial globe.*" (*Ibid.*)

The italics are his; and it thus appears that after Justinian—in other words, after the year of Christ, 565, the Monogram of Christ, the CHI-RO, vanished, and the Heathen emblem of Venus, the *Crux Ansata*, took its place on the banner, and in the hand of the Roman emperors.

Thus early in the Church the emblem of *Christ* was superseded by the emblem of *Venus*.

The *Pagan* and *Christian Cross.*

If Paganism had not at first familiarised men from infancy to the *Cross*, an emblem so polluted and disgusting as *a gibbet* could hardly have found the favour which it did through the Christian world after the fourth century. Once in vogue, with the tendency which for two thousand years prior to the successors of CONSTANTINE the human family had shown towards its culture, no wonder that it has subsequently maintained its ground. Emperors, empresses, and kings set the example, priests and bishops adopted the Pagano-Christian sign. These were the rulers of men. What wonder, then, if flocks followed the shepherds—if the ruled imitated the rulers !

The translator of Zœckler, in his preface (xl.), however, justly observes, " That *the early Christians* shrank from directly *depicting the instrument* of our Lord's passion is well known."

XXX.

BUT more directly to our matter in hand.

Up, then, to the time of CONSTANTINE (that is, for the *three first centuries*, after Christ) the Cross generally remained, what it had been for ages upon ages, *a purely Heathen emblem.*

And a Heathen emblem it seemingly continued for the best part of another hundred years, *i.e.*, up to about A.D. 400. And such in India it yet is.

CONSTANTINE, we have seen, did not adopt *the Cross.* He adopted *two letters.* He made *them* his sign. One letter happened to be a cross letter, X. (*Chi*), which was converted, later in time, by superstition into a Cross, as below (Fig. 3).

To this Greek letter *Ch* (X) CONSTANTINE added the Greek *Ro* (P) forming CHR, a *Monogram* of the *first part of the title* CHR-ist (Fig. 1).

CONSTANTINE, mark, did not choose the letter X (*Chi*) *because* it was a *Cross,* but because it happened to be the *first letter of the title,* CH-rist.

Observe, now, the order of the adoption of the Heathen emblem into the Christian Church.

1. We have the *Chi-Ro* of Constantine *cir.* A.D. 312 (Fig. 1).

2. The *Chi*, no longer *a letter,* but formed into

a *Cross*, the *Ro* answering to our P, remaining in its
original position (Fig. 2).

3. The *Ro* rejected, and the X (*Chi*), changed
into a *Greek* Cross (*the Cross of Bacchus*) *alone
retained* (Fig. 3).

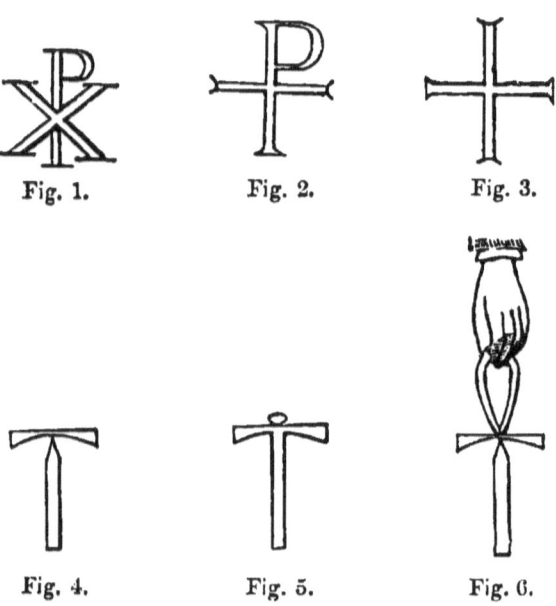

Fig. 1.   Fig. 2.   Fig. 3.

Fig. 4.   Fig. 5.   Fig. 6.

4. The Heathen *Tau* (T), as used in Heathen
India, and in Egypt adopted, probably, because re-
sembling the supposed form of the Cross of Christ,
as well as to avoid persecution, as before referred to.
(Fig. 4.)

5. The same *Tau* (Fig. 5), surmounted with a
roundel (probably the sacred egg, a Heathen emblem
of the goddess Nature, the *productive* principle),

which assimilates the Pagan sign yet more to the *Latin* Cross. (The generative principle is elsewhere noticed.)

6. The same *Tau* with a handle (Fig. 6), the *crux unsata,* or *handled* Cross (from *ansa, a handle*), as seen usually in the hands of the gods of India and of Egypt.

The three Crosses following are from an extensive

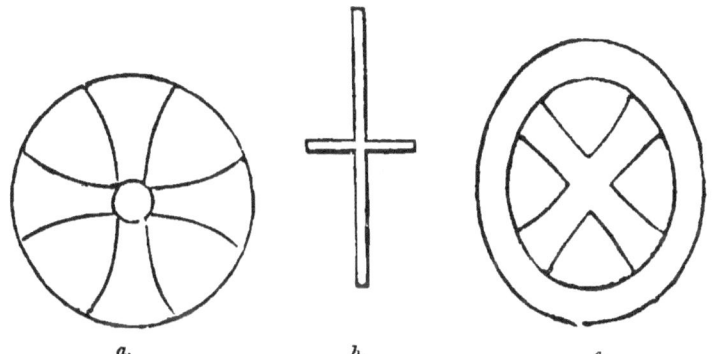

a. *b.* *c.*
Crosses from an ancient Egyptian writing from Thebes.

ancient Egyptian writing, a copy of which was given me in Egypt by a gentleman of the name of Murray, in 1872. It is now with Dr. Birch in the British Museum for the use of students.

As to the three Crosses, the learned doctor informs me that he considers *a,* to be Christian ; *b,* perhaps the Cross above alluded to by Christian writers ; *c,* a cross-cake, or ornament of a building.

At Philæ, on the north border of Nubia, close to "the tower of Syene," now *Assouan,* in the great temple there, I saw several Crosses cut into the walls, and picked up a piece of one, now by me, with the paint yet fresh on it. They are the shape of *a*, except that the blades are oval.

a, is the exact form of a R.C. medal, of recent times, figured in Picart, and now, I believe, in common use.

Mr. H. D. Ward's little work on the Cross (Nisbet, 1871) is well worthy of attention.

XXXI.

AND thus in the space of 300 years—from CONSTANTINE to PHOCAS—we see *Christ's monogram*, the *Chi-Ro* (only, mind, a human invention) go out, and the *Heathen Cross* come in.

As to the *Tau* being *used in the Old Testament*—whether for the uplifting the serpent in the wilderness, or for marking the saints in Ezekiel ix.—being used as having a *symbolical reference to the Cross* of Christ—that is mere fancy.

In regard, further, to the *Chi-Ro*, it appears only *occasionally* in BARONIUS during the period above named; it went out of use.

No. It was the adaptation of the Pagan Cross that found favour with a people which had turned back—back unto Paganism—the degraded followers of the HOLY JESUS, who were soon by the righteous judgment of God to be given up for their idolatry to the avenging scimitar of ISLAM, and swept by the ferocious OTTOMANS, *idol-haters*, from the face of the earth.

Reader, let us also take warning, and "flee from idolatry."

Finally, as to "*the Sign of the Cross.*"

Here is the use of it, "if it be made with faith in the Divine mercy, and merits of Christ," as we are informed in "the Christian Doctrine"—then,—

"This sign is made to arm oneself against every temptation of the devil, because the devil is afraid of this sign, and flies from it. Oftentimes, through means of this sign of the holy Cross, man escapes many dangers, spiritual and temporal."

Where, one would like to know, does the writer learn that the devil *fears* and *flies from* this charm?

Does *the Scripture* so teach us?

And with an example of the uselessness of "*the*

Sign of the Cross" practically applied we conclude this FRAGMENT.

Not far from the gambling-house at Monte Carlo, (Monaco) there is a rock, of about 300 feet in height, overlooking the sea, famous for its suicides. It is called "Bastion des Décavés," the precipice of the cleared out, or ruined. Formerly, it was a defence against pirates, now it is the last refuge of the destitute, who have been plundered by the land-pirates of Monaco.

" Near the bastion, on the Promenade S. Martin," writes one, " I was walking, March 19, 1873, at 6 p.m., when I perceived a man standing upright on the precipice. He made *the sign of the Cross,* and as he saw me advance, leaped into the sea. When I reached the spot he had disappeared."

The sign of the Cross, and, death! Superstition, and self-murder!

THE END.

BILLING AND SONS, PRINTERS, GUILDFORD, SURREY.

Extracts from Articles CROSS, CRUCIFIX, CONSTANTINE,
in Lichtenberger's " Encyclopédie des Sciences religieuses."
Paris, Sandoz, 1878.

THE CROSS.

"THE CROSS is found in all heathen countries from the
highest antiquity. As to when and how it was adopted by
the Christians as a symbol of their redemption, recent archæo-
logical discoveries oblige us to leave the common tradition.
The most ancient Christian monuments, especially those of
the Catacombs of Rome, reveal that the Cross, properly so
called, did not in iconography appear regularly (*régulièrement*),
but at the beginning of the fifth century. . . . . The
Cross, then, is not early shown on the monuments. Opinions
do not vary on this incontestable fact, but only on the cause
of it."

THE CRUCIFIX.

"THE CRUCIFIX showed itself yet very much later than the
Cross (*bien plus tard encore*). . . . Scenes of martyrdom
originally are not found in monuments of Christian art, either
in the Catacombs or elsewhere, a strong reason why one should
less expect to meet, explicitly represented, the punishment of
the Master. Such representations were not made till the
eighth century, when the *Byzantine Monks*, under persecution,
induced (for their own glorification) a certain admiration for
scenes of blood. To them are attributed the execution of the
little ivory Diptychs, painted with representations of the crucifixion of Christ, a thing clearly, before, unknown at Rome."

The reader will observe that by far the earliest specimen
extant of the CRUCIFIX is the "Graffito Blasfemo" of p. 51.

CONSTANTINE.

"CONSTANTINE, as to paganism, took care his last days should not be troubled about it. It is certain he never forbade the worship of idols; he raised up the pagan temple of Concord; he permitted the diviners to consult the entrails of victims. Let us add, that Constantine disgraced his private life by many odious crimes. He strangled Licinius after having pardoned him; the young son of his rival, aged twelve, was also put to death by his order. He beheaded his son Crispus, giving faith to a false accusation of his wife Fausta, whom he then suffocated in a stove. In brief, this man, who only consented to receive baptism in the article of death, appears to us to have been, before all things, an able politician and an impassioned autocrat of unity."

"As to the miracle of the year 312 [the Cross], it is *absolutely contradicted* by that which preceded it. It is not even possible to admit the natural fact [clouds] supposed by Neander. The leaning of Constantine towards Christianity only depended on his political interests, and appeared for the first time in 313. For the rest, this miracle, it is time to say, *has no serious historical foundation.*"—*Encyclopédie des Sciences religieuses*, par Lichtenberger, vol. iii. p. 391.

WORSHIP:

WHAT IT IS NOT, AND WHAT IT IS.

IN A LETTER TO THE VERY REV. THE DEAN OF BRISTOL.

BY MOURANT BROCK, M.A.

By Book Post 12 of these Leaflets can be sent for a halfpenny.

Price, Two Shillings per Hundred. Postage, 5d.

SHORT PAPERS ON THE SACRAMENTS.

BY MOURANT BROCK, M.A.,

Formerly Vicar of Christ Church, Clifton.

Addressed to the Right Rev. Bishop Anderson.

LONDON: HAMILTON, ADAMS, AND CO., 32, PATERNOSTER ROW.

BRISTOL: I. E. CHILLCOTT, 26, CLARE STREET.